RUSSIAN RIVER
WINE ROAD

"Tasting Along the Wine Road" Cookbook

A Wine & Food Affair

*A collection of recipes from the wineries of
The Russian River Wine Road in The Alexander Valley,
The Dry Creek Valley, and The Russian River Valley in
Northwest Sonoma County, California*

"A Wine & Food Affair" in partnership with

A custom cookbook
published by
The Hoffman Press
Santa Rosa, California

Cover illustration and page drawings by Pam Lewis

CONTENTS

Introduction

Along the Russian River Wine Road in northwest Sonoma County, California, a lot of our time is spent thinking about, talking about, producing, and occasionally drinking wine.

Most of us work in the wine business because we enjoy wine, hospitality and introducing people to our area, our wineries and—our wines. Our second love is food. Especially pairing wine and food. Endless hours are spent pairing our wines with locally grown and other foods to create delicious, and many times simple, meals; then sharing these meals with friends and family.

Our passion for wine and food prompted us to create *A Wine & Food Affair*, an event that showcases the wineries and wines of the Russian River Wine Road and pairs wine with food. Invariably, when we serve food in the wineries we are asked for the recipes, and many of the wineries have printed up recipes to give to their customers.

This led us to the idea of producing our own cookbook featuring the recipes of our member wineries.The cookbook is given to each attendee of *A Wine & Food Affair*.

We hope you enjoy the wines and recipes in these books as much as we enjoyed creating them.

A tip of the glass from us to you!

The Russian River Wine Road

The Russian River Wine Road

For over 20 years the Russian River Wine Road has been an association of wineries and lodgings in the Alexander Valley, Dry Creek Valley, and Russian River Valley appellations of northwest Sonoma County, California. The Wine Road now consists of over 70 wineries and 38 lodgings. From the Pacific Ocean and the redwoods through the Russian River Valley to the benchlands of Dry Creek Valley and rolling hills over-looking the Alexander Valley, are wineries and vine-yards.

Grapes have been grown and wine has been made in northwest Sonoma County for over 130 years. The Russian River Wine Road has wineries that have been in business (with a short break for Prohibition) for over 100 years. Some winery families have been in the business for four or five generations, while other winery owners left careers in such fields as engineering, retailing, medicine and finance to plant grapes and make wines.

Some of the finest wines in the world are made in this region. With a variety of soil types and climates, we are able to grow over 25 different varieties of grapes, all of which are used in the production of spectacular wines.

You can also find lodgings to suit any taste from B&B's housed in 100-year-old Victorian mansions to new inns and motels. In addition to our wines the members of the Wine Road are known for their hospitality and friendliness.

Come for a visit. You're always welcome.

Participating Wineries in *The Wine & Food Affair*

Alderbrook Winery
 Armida Winery
  Belvedere Winery & Vineyards
  Blackstone Winery
   Canyon Road Winery
    Chateau Souverain
     Christopher Creek Winery
      Davis Bynum Winery
      De Natale Vineyards
       Dry Creek Vineyard
        Everett Ridge Winery
       Field Stone Winery & Vineyard
      Forchini Vineyards & Winery
    Geyser Peak Winery
     Hanna Winery – Alexander Valley & Santa Rosa
   Hop Kiln Winery
 Kendall-Jackson Wine Center
Korbel Champagne Cellars
  Lake Sonoma Winery
   Lambert Bridge Winery
    Mark West Estate Winery
    Martini & Prati Winery
     Mazzocco Vineyards
      Mill Creek Vineyards
       Optima Wine Cellars
        Pedroncelli Winery
         Pezzi King Vineyards
          Sausal Winery
           Sebastopol Vineyards
            Simi Winery
             Sommer Vineyards & Winery
            Rodney Strong Vineyards
           Taft Street Winery
          Tasting On The Plaza
         F. Teldeschi Winery
        Topolos at Russian River Vineyards
        Trentadue Winery
      White Oak Vineyards & Winery
     Windsor Vineyards
      Yoakim Bridge Vineyards & Winery

THE WINE REGIONS OF NORTHWEST SONOMA COUNTY
CALIFORNIA

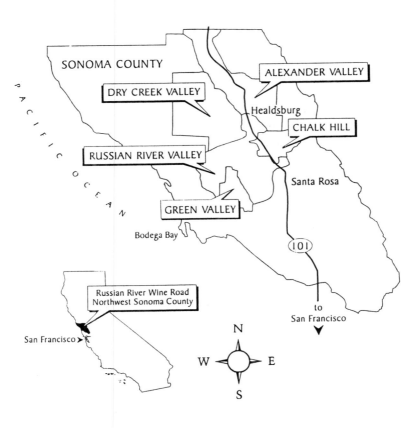

9

The Russian River Wine Road Today

The Russian River Wine Road has many projects to make it easy for visitors to visit the area. Best known for the Russian River Wine Road Map, which has been published for many years, the Wine Road has expanded into many areas, producing three events annually and creating a web site. The newest venture is a club for our customers and visitors known as *"RoadRunners."*

The Map
The Russian River Wine Road Map is available free simply by calling (800) 723-6336. The map includes information on all our winery and lodging members, plus special events and the area.

Winter Wineland
Held the next-to-last weekend of January, before the Super Bowl, Winter Wineland offers a bright, fun weekend of wine tasting, information, talks by wine-makers, vineyard and winery tours.

Barrel Tasting
Held the first full weekend in March, this is the longest-running free wine event. Barrel Tasting has been held for over 20 years. It offers an opportunity to taste wines from the barrel to purchase futures—many times at discount prices—of wine that is not yet released.

A Wine & Food Affair, A Tasting Along the Wine Road
Held mid-May, the weekend after Mother's Day A wonderful weekend in the Alexander, Dry Creek and Russian River valleys. A premier wine and food event, at which attendees can savor wine and food pairing at many wineries. The recipes prepared by the wineries are in this cookbook.

The Web Site
www.wineroad.com

The Web Site keeps you up to date with everything that is going on along the Russian River Wine Road. You may download information about the wineries, the Wine Road and events, or purchase tickets for events, extra copies of the cookbook, or find out about RoadRunners. Everything you want to know about the Wine Road is available on the Web Site.

RoadRunners

RoadRunners is an opportunity for wine and food lovers to become a part of the Wine Road. Meet and mingle with the winemakers, owners and winery staff. Taste the wines and participate in exclusive events. We invite you to join. There are many benefits to becoming a member:

- A RoadRunner T-shirt.
- Newsletters with information regarding wines, wineries, and events along the Wine Road.
- "Road Trip"—a special event held for RoadRunners.
- Discount on tickets to events sponsored by RRWR.
- Special considerations at selected wineries and lodgings.
- First option to purchase tickets for the Wine Road events.

Varietal Wines Produced Along the Wine Road

Red Wines

Barbera
Carignane
Cabernet Franc
Cabernet Sauvignon
Cinsault
Gamay Beaujolais
Late Harvest Zinfandel
Merlot
Meritage
Mourvédre
Petite Syrah
Pinot Noir
Port
Sangiovese
Syrah
Valdiguié
Zinfandel

White Wines

Chardonnay
Chenin Blanc
Fumé Blanc
Gewürztraminer
Late Harvest Sauvignon
Muscat
Riesling
Sauvignon Blanc
Semillon
Sparkling Wine (Champagne)
Viognier
White Zinfandel

APPETIZERS
AND
LIGHT FOODS

Roasted Eggplant Sandwich with Provolone and Fennel Salamé

1 small uniform eggplant
1/4 pound Italian Provolone cheese, grated
4 slices of fennel salamé
1 egg, beaten with 2 tablespoons water
1/2 cup seasoned bread crumbs
2 tablespoons extra virgin olive oil

Preheat oven to 375 degrees.

Slice eggplant into 1/4-inch rounds (cross-wise). Lay slices on flat surface and cover half of them with grated cheese and 1 slice of fennel salamé. Cover with other half of eggplant slices.

Dip the sandwich into egg and cover with bread crumbs. Place on cookie sheet that has been oiled or covered with foil or parchment. Season with salt and pepper. Drizzle oil over top of each sandwich.

Bake 35 to 45 minutes until sandwiches are browned and eggplant is sufficiently cooked.

Serves 4.

Serve with Sausal 1996 Zinfandel.

Sausal Winery

Grilled Duck-Apple Sausage with Balsamic Onions

1 pound duck-apple sausage (about 4 sausages)
2 white onions, sliced
2 yellow onions, sliced
1/2 cup balsamic vinegar
2 tablespoons olive oil
Focaccia or crostini

Slice onions 1/8 inch thick and separate rings. Heat olive oil in a pan on medium-high heat, sauté onions until they begin to soften. Turn heat down and slowly cook onions, stirring occasionally, until they begin to turn golden brown (about 15 minutes). Add vinegar and continue cooking until dark brown and caramelized (about 5 minutes more).

Grill sausage on medium-high grill, until just cooked through (about 10 to 12 minutes). Slice sausages one inch thick and serve on focaccia squares or crostini topped with onions.

Makes 20 appetizers.

Serve with Martini & Prati Tesoro d'Elmo.

Martini & Prati Winery

Eggplant Roulades with Proscuitto

1 eggplant
12 thin slices of Provolone cheese
12 slices of proscuitto
1/4 cup olive oil
1 teaspoon minced garlic

Slice eggplant crosswise into 1/4-inch thick rounds. (Try to use a large enough eggplant to get 12 slices.) Salt lightly and drain between sheets of paper towels for one-half hour or more (place something heavy on top to weigh it down).

On a medium grill, grill eggplant slices until tender. Set aside to cool.

Preheat oven to 325 degrees. On each eggplant round, stack with one slice of Provolone followed by a slice of proscuitto. Roll into a log and secure with a toothpick. Bake in 325-degree oven just until cheese melts. Serve immediately.

Makes 12 roulades.

Serve with Martini & Prati Reserve Russian River Valley Zinfandel.

Recipe created by Chef Barbara Hom for
Martini & Prati Winery

Pissaladiére (Focaccia with Onions, Olives and Anchovies)

DOUGH
1 package dry yeast
Olive oil
3 cups flour
1 tablespoon salt
1 tablespoon cornmeal

TOPPING
1/4 cup olive oil
2 to 3 onions, depending on size
Salt and pepper
2 sprigs each thyme, marjoram and rosemary
1/3 cup nicoise olives
12 anchovy filets
1/2 cup red wine

<u>Dough</u>: Dissolve yeast in 1 cup warm water, 5 minutes. Add 1/4 cup oil. Combine flour and salt in a medium bowl; add yeast mixture, stirring well. Turn dough onto floured board, knead until smooth and elastic. Return to oiled bowl. Cover and let rise 1 hour.

Topping: Heat oil in large pan. Slice onions thinly. Season with salt and pepper. Add herbs and cook, covered, over low heat for 45 minutes. Uncover and add 1/2 cup red wine; cook until liquid evaporates and the onions have the consistency of jam, 30 to 40 minutes. Let cool.

Preheat oven to 450 degrees. Roll dough into thin rectangle. Dust top of dough rectangle with cornmeal. Cover, let rise for 30 minutes. Spread onion mixture, olives and anchovies over top. Bake 15 to 20 minutes. Serve warm with minced fresh herbs on top. Cut in squares.

Makes 10 to 15 small pieces.

Serve with Martin Ray '97 Pinot Noir California.

Blackstone Winery

Polenta Sandwich with Mushroom Duxelle Filling

MUSHROOM DUXELLE FILLING
6 cups button or crimini mushrooms, chopped
    very fine or minced in food processor
2 cups portabello mushrooms, chopped very
    fine or minced in food processor
2 tablespoons olive oil
1 teaspoon garlic, minced
1/2 cup white wine
1/4 pound mild white cheese, any variety

POLENTA
1 cup dry polenta
1 cup cream
2 cups chicken stock
4 ounces butter
2 teaspoons fresh garlic, chopped

Cook mushroom filling first. Heat sauté pan with olive oil. Once oil is smoking, add mushrooms. Cook until water in mushrooms has evaporated. Add white wine and garlic and cook until almost dry. Set aside. Do not let cool.

In large pot, add butter and all liquid ingredients. Heat until it reaches boiling point; lower heat immediately. Whisk in polenta until mixture begins thickening. Add garlic. Stir frequently for 10 to 15 minutes until polenta thickens to oatmeal consistency.

Butter bottom of 9 x 13-inch baking dish and spread half of the polenta evenly on the bottom.

Sprinkle mushroom mixture and cheese evenly over entire polenta and top with remaining polenta. Cool, cut and serve.

Makes approximately 25 to 30 servings.

Serve with Chateau Souverain Chardonnay.

by Martin Courtman, Executive Chef
Chateau Souverain

White Bean and Sun-Dried Crostini

2 baguettes, day-old
Olive oil (optional)
1/2 recipe White Bean Purée (see recipe below)
2 cups minced sun-dried tomatoes packed in oil,
**   drained**
Optional garnish: chopped fresh herbs such as
**   thyme, parsley, oregano**

Slice baguettes into thin rounds. Brush lightly with olive oil, if desired, and bake in a 325-degree oven until lightly browned, about 15 minutes. (Times will vary depending on the dryness of the bread.) Put aside.

Mix the minced sun-dried tomatoes into the white bean purée and spread on toasts. Sprinkle with chopped fresh herbs and serve.

A few years ago I would have said that you couldn't remove fat from a cuisine that was meant to be served with wine, as the fat was necessary to balance the acid in the wine. Having researched low-fat cooking, I now know there are some ingredients that can imitate fat on the palate. I place beans on the top of that list. I use this purée in place of mashed potatoes or as a topping for crostini.

White Bean Purée

1 pound white beans, picked over
1 large onion, roughly chopped
4 large cloves garlic, peeled and smashed
**2 tomatoes, peeled and roughly chopped (option-
al)4 cups vegetable stock (or 2 cups canned stock
and**
  2 cups water)
Salt and freshly ground pepper to taste

Combine beans with vegetables in a deep pot and add vegetable stock to cover. Bring to a boil, then reduce to a simmer and cook until beans are tender, about one hour. (Times can vary quite a bit depending on the age of the beans, so test a bean occasionally to monitor.)

Add stock as necessary so that beans remain just covered by liquid. When you run out of stock, use water.

When beans are tender, strain them, reserving the cooking liquid. Transfer to a food processor, add 1/3 cup of the cooking liquid and purée. Add more liquid, if necessary, until the beans are completely puréed but still hold their shape in a spoon.

Makes 80 to 100 pieces.

Serve with Simi Shiraz.

Recipe by Mary Evely, Executive Chef
Simi Winery

Ricotta Cheese with Rosemary and Olive Oil

8 ounces ricotta cheese
1/4 teaspoon kosher salt
1/8 teaspoon freshly ground pepper
Pinch of finely crushed rosemary
2 brine-cured green olives, minced
2 teaspoons extra virgin olive oil

Spread ricotta in an even layer on a plate. Sprinkle with salt, pepper, rosemary and minced olives. Dribble the olive oil evenly over the cheese.

Serve with crackers or thinly sliced Italian bread.

Serves 6 to 8.

Serve with Pedroncelli Fumé Blanc or Zinfandel Rosé.

Pedroncelli Winery

Curried Turkey on Crostini

2 cups roasted turkey breast (diced)
1/4 cup golden raisins
2 stalks celery, diced
1/4 medium red onion, minced
1/4 cup mayonnaise
1/4 teaspoon curry powder
1 baguette

Mix together turkey, raisins, celery, and onion. Mix curry powder into mayonnaise. Then mix curried mayonnaise into turkey mixture. (*Curry will get stronger with time. You may need more curry if eating immediately.*)

Slice baguette into 1-inch rounds and toast before serving. Spread curried turkey mixture on each round.
Makes 15 to 20 appetizers.

Serve with Windsor Private Reserve Pinot Noir RRV or Windsor 1997 Sonoma County Gewürtztraminer.

Recipe by Plaza Street Cafe for
Windsor Vineyards

Caponata

6 cups eggplant, diced
3 tablespoons salt
6 tablespoons extra virgin olive oil
1 cup red onion, diced
6 cloves garlic, peeled and sliced thin
1 cup tomato sauce
3 anchovy filets, rinsed, dried and chopped fine
1/2 cup golden raisins
1 tablespoon each fresh thyme and parsley, chopped
1 cup red wine
1 ounce Balsamic vinegar

Sprinkle salt over eggplant and toss together in a bowl. Cover eggplant with paper towels and place a heavy weight on top. Set aside for 30 minutes. Drain eggplant of excess water. Pour 3 tablespoons olive oil in a sauté pan and place over medium-high heat along with onions. Cook until caramelized. Remove from heat and set aside.

Pour remaining olive oil in pan and return to heat. Sauté garlic until crispy. Combine red wine, tomato paste, Balsamic vinegar, water, and anchovies. Add this mixture to pan. Cook over medium heat for approximately 10 minutes. With the pot on medium heat, add eggplant, onions, and raisins. Cook for 10 more minutes and remove from heat. Add chopped herbs and season with salt and pepper.

Serves 10 to 12.

Serve with Stonestreet Pinot Noir.

Kendall-Jackson Vineyards

Saganaki

This is one of our most requested recipes at Topolos Russian River Vineyard. It's a rough and sizzling fondue, not smooth and creamy like the French version. Flamed with Metaxa or Brandy at the table, it starts any meal off with a flourish.

8 ounces Kasseri cheese, grated
1 teaspoon red wine vinegar
1 teaspoon lemon juice
1/2 teaspoon Greek oregano
1-1/2 tablespoons Metaxa or Brandy

We use a cow's milk Kasseri made in Wisconsin. It has a pleasant Cheddar texture with a distinct nutty Parmesan tang. The Greek Kasseri is often too sharp for American tastes and varies in quality.

Use a heavy skillet, cast iron or aluminum, about six or eight inches in diameter. Melt the cheese slowly over medium low heat, stirring occasionally. When mostly melted, raise the flame to high, stir in the red wine vinegar and lemon juice, sprinkle the top with the oregano. Have a match ready! Pour the brandy around the outer edge and ignite. Hoopa!

Serve with crusty bread.
                    Yield approximately 1-1/2 to 2 cups.

Serve with a hearty and spicy red like our Russian River Vineyard Piner Heights Zinfandel.

Topolos at Russian River Vineyards

Smoked Salmon Tapenade

4 large Roma tomatoes, seeded and diced
1/4 cup green onions, chopped
2 tablespoons parsley, minced
2 tablespoons cilantro, minced
4 ounces smoked salmon, diced
3 tablespoons olive oil
2 tablespoons capers, with a little juice
1 lemon juiced
1 lime, juiced
Salt and pepper to taste

Mix all the above ingredients, blending well. Serve on croutons, or in baby potatoes that have been boiled, chilled, and halved.

Makes 25 portions.

Serve with Pezzi King Sauvignon Blanc.

Lois Weinstein for
Pezzi King Vineyards

Yoakim Polenta

This polenta was created as an accompaniment to our "Yoakim Smokin' Chili." It is to be served warm in a bowl with the chili on top. Enjoy!

8 cups chicken stock, the richer the better
2 cups polenta, as fresh as possible
2 cups Cheddar cheese, grated
2 cups Jack cheese, grated
4 tablespoons butter
1 cup fresh cilantro, chopped, or 2 tablespoons
  dried, if fresh cilantro is unavailable
2 tablespoons garlic flakes
1 tablespoon ground cumin
2 teaspoons salt
1 teaspoon ground black pepper

Bring chicken stock, garlic, and salt and pepper to a boil. Gradually add polenta, stirring constantly. Reduce heat to simmer; stir frequently for approximately 20 minutes. Blend in butter, cheeses and cilantro. When creamy and thick, pour into a 17-1/4 x 11-1/2 x 1-inch sheet pan that has been sprayed with Pam, or buttered. Let cool; cut into 4-1/2 x 4-1/2-inch squares.

Serves 15.

Serve with Yoakim Bridge Premier Release Dry Creek Valley Zinfandel.

Yoakim Bridge Vineyard & Winery

Goat Cheese Napoleons with Three-Onion Marmalade

FOR THE NAPOLEON:
1 sheet puff pastry (available in the frozen food
   section)
1 cup goat cheese
1/2 cup cream cheese, room temperature
1/2 teaspoon nutmeg
1/2 teaspoon vanilla

FOR THE MARMALADE:
2 white onions, peeled and sliced 1/8-inch thick
2 yellow onions, peeled and sliced 1/8-inch thick
2 leeks, white part only, peeled and sliced 1/8-inch
   thick
1/2 cup orange juice mixed with 1/4 cup sugar
1/4 cup olive oil

Make marmalade: Heat the olive oil on medium-high, sauté the onions and leeks until they begin to soften. Turn heat to low and add orange juice mixture, 2 tablespoons at a time, every few minutes until gone. Continue cooking until onions and leeks are brown and caramelized, about 30 minutes.

Make the Napoleon: Lay the pastry on a work surface, prick with a fork, and cut into 1-inch x 2-inch diamond shapes. Bake on a baking sheet according to package directions (approximately 12 minutes in a 450-degree oven). Remove diamonds from oven and let cool.

In a mixing bowl, blend together goat cheese, cream cheese, nutmeg and vanilla. Split diamonds in half, spread with goat cheese mixture, followed by a dollop of the marmalade, and top with the other half.

Makes 12 appetizers.

Serve with Mark West Russian River Chardonnay.

Recipe created especially by Chef Barbara Hom for
Mark West Estate Winery

Tzatziki

Here is another recipe from Topolos Russian River Vineyard. A simple dip for bread that is very low in salt and fat, it makes an excellent alternative to butter.

2 medium cucumbers
2 cups plain yogurt
2 teaspoons garlic, minced
Dash or two of white pepper

Peel the cucumber and cut in half the long way. Use the tip of a spoon to scoop and scrape the seeds out. Discard the seeds. What you end up with looks like a pair of dugout canoes. Grate the cucumber or use a food processor to chop it very finely. Put the grated or chopped cucumber in a sieve and squeeze vigorously to remove all water. You could also put the cucumber in a towel and wring the juice out.

If you want to make a very thick yogurt such as they have in Greece, line a sieve with cheesecloth and drain the yogurt overnight in the refrigerator. In Greece they use a pillowcase (and often skip the refrigeration!)

Combine the cucumber meat, yogurt and garlic in a bowl. Add white pepper and more garlic to taste.
Makes 2-1/2 cups.

Serve with Russian River Vineyard Piner Heights Zinfandel.

Topolos at Russian River Vineyards

Bay Shrimp Salad Topping

2 cups bay shrimp, cooked
1 cup mayonnaise
1 tablespoon horseradish
2 teaspoons Dijon mustard
1 teaspoon dill seed
2 tablespoons green onions, chopped
1 tablespoon lemon juice

Chop bay shrimp and toss with the remaining ingredients in a bowl. Chill for two hours. Serve with your favorite bread, crackers or toast.

Serves 10 to 12.

Serve with Lambert Bridge 1997 Chardonnay.

Lambert Bridge Winery

Basil and Asiago Focaccia with Roasted Red Pepper Pesto

4 cups flour
Pinch of salt
1 tablespoon yeast (1-1/4 package active dry yeast)
1 teaspoon sugar
1 cup warm milk (110F. or 45C.)
1/4 cup extra-virgin olive oil, plus extra for brushing
1 tablespoon fresh basil, chopped
2 tablespoons fresh grated asiago/romano cheese
Coarse sea salt
Roasted red pepper pesto* (recipe below)

Sift flour and salt into a large bowl. In a small bowl, dissolve yeast and sugar in milk. Let stand 5 to 10 minutes until frothy. Stir in the 1/4 cup olive oil. Using a wooden spoon, gradually beat yeast mixture into flour mixture to give a soft, but not sticky, dough. Knead on a lightly floured surface 5 minutes until smooth and elastic. Place in an oiled medium-sized bowl, cover and let rise in a warm place about 40 minutes until doubled in size.

Turn out onto a lightly floured surface and knead 5 minutes.

Oil a baking sheet. Roll out dough to a large circle about 1/2-inch thick and transfer to baking sheet. Brush dough with olive oil, sprinkle with basil, asiago cheese, and sea salt. Lightly press ingredients into surface. With your finger make deep indentations over surface. Let rise 25 minutes. Preheat oven to 450 degrees.

Bake in preheated oven 20 to 25 minutes, until golden. Brush top again with small amount of olive oil.

Cut into squares or rectangles, spooning the roasted red pepper pesto onto each piece of focaccia. (Red pepper pesto recipe follows.)

*Roasted Red Pepper Pesto

**5 red bell peppers or 1 16-ounce jar "Mezzetta" roasted
 red peppers
1/4 cup fresh basil
1/4 cup pine nuts
1/3 cup parmesan cheese
1/4 cup extra-virgin olive oil
1 tablespoon garlic, chopped
1 tablespoon balsamic vinegar
Salt and pepper**

Roast peppers in oven until all sides of peppers are charred. Immediately put peppers into cold water to cool. Peel charred skins off cooled peppers, remove core and seeds.

Add peppers, basil, garlic, pine nuts, and vinegar, to food processor or blender. Purée ingredients while slowly adding olive oil (about 30 seconds). Blend in parmesan cheese, 10 seconds. Season with salt and pepper to taste.

Yield–topping for 1 focaccia.
This recipe makes 1 focaccia approximately 13"x15".

Serve with Forchini Vineyards 1997 Zinfandel, Dry Creek Valley, Estate Bottled.

Forchini Vineyards

Salmon Mousse

1 can red salmon, cleaned of bones and skin
8 ounces cream cheese (light style works well)
1/2 lemon, juiced
Freshly ground black pepper to taste
Fresh dill, capers and chopped red onion for
    garnish

In a food processor, combine first four ingredients. Refrigerate for 2 to 4 hours or overnight. Mound onto serving platter and garnish. Serve with water crackers or thinly sliced sourdough baguettes.

Serves 8 to 12.

Serve with F. Johnson Chardonnay or Fumé Blanc.

Pedroncelli Winery

Asparagus and Prosciutto Rolls

24 spears medium asparagus
8 thin (but not paper-thin) slices prosciutto
1 small head frisee or curly endive
Lemon oil
Freshly ground black pepper
Optional: Parmesan shavings

Snap off the tough ends of the asparagus and trim spears to even lengths. Cook in boiling, salted water for 6 to 7 minutes, or until the asparagus is bright green and crisp-tender. Lift out with tongs and let drain and cool to room temperature.

Arrange a bundle of 3 spears of asparagus lengthwise on a slice of prosciutto and roll up. Cut horizontally into 4 or 5 even pieces. Tuck a sprig of frisee or curly endive into the top of each piece. Sprinkle tops with a little lemon oil and a grinding of black pepper.

For a plated first course cut the bundles into uneven lengths for visual interest and stand a group in the middle of a plate. You can be a little more generous with the lemon oil, and scatter Parmesan shavings over the top.

Serves 4 to 6 as main course,
or 32 to 40 appetizers.

Serve with Simi Sendal (Reserve-Style Sauvignon Blanc)

Recipe by Mary Evely, Executive Chef
Simi Winery

Ceviche

**3/4 pound sea bass or snapper, cut into 1-inch
   cubes**
3/4 pound scallops (if large, cut into small pieces)
1 pound bay shrimp
1 cup lime juice
1/2 cup White Oak Sauvignon Blanc
1 cup green onions, chopped
1/4 cup yellow bell pepper, seeded and minced
1 large, fresh tomato, chopped
1/4 cup fresh cilantro, chopped
1/4 cup olive oil
3 Jalapeño peppers, seeded and finely chopped
Salt and pepper to taste

Combine fish and scallops in large bowl. Toss with the lime juice and refrigerate overnight. Drain, reserving 1/2 the liquid.

Add the bay shrimp, white wine, onion, yellow pepper, tomato, cilantro, olive oil and jalapeños. Toss and allow to marinate at least 1 hour.

Season with salt and pepper and the reserved liquid. Serve with avocado slices and tortilla chips.

Makes 8 servings.

Serve with White Oak Sauvignon Blanc.

Recipe by Gail Paquette for
White Oak Vineyards and Winery

Smoked Salmon Rounds

16-ounces smoked salmon
16-ounce package cream cheese, cubed
1 tablespoon dill,chopped
2 tablespoons small capers
1/2 cup shallots, chopped
1/2 tablespoon garlic, chopped
1 tablespoon extra-virgin olive oil
1/4 cup Marsala wine
Salt and pepper to taste

Heat small skillet, medium-high. Add olive oil. When skillet and oil are hot, add shallots and garlic. Stirring frequently, cook shallots and garlic until golden. Add Marsala wine. Reduce wine until there is almost no liquid remaining. Set aside to cool.

In a food processor or blender, add remaining ingredients with cooled shallots. Blend until ingredients are thoroughly mixed, but slightly chunky.

Serve spread over cucumber or cracker rounds, or piped onto whole mushrooms. You may also serve this as a dip.

Makes 30 to 40 appetizers.

Serve with Forchini Vineyards 1997 Pinot Noir, Russian River Valley Estate-grown.

Recipe by Steve Carlson for
Forchini Vineyards

Redwood Hill Farms Goat Cheese Tart with Lemon and Rosemary

CRUST
1-1/2 cups flour
1/4 teaspoon salt
6 tablespoons butter
2 tablespoons Gorgonzola
1/4 cup ice water

FILLING
4 ounces Ricotta cheese
8 ounces Redwood Hill Farms Chevre
1 egg yolk
2 tablespoons fresh rosemary
1 tablespoon flour
1/2 teaspoon coarse ground black pepper
Zest of 1 lemon

Crust: Combine flour and salt in food processor; pulse. Add butter and gorgonzola; pulse to coarse crumbs. Add water slowly until ball forms. Wrap and chill 3 hours. Roll 1/8-inch thick and place in 10-inch tart pan. Prebake with foil and weights at 375 degrees for 10 minutes. Remove foil and bake another 10 minutes. Cool before filling.

Filling: Combine ingredients; add to shell. Bake at 375 degrees for 25 to 30 minutes. Garnish with julienned roasted peppers and rosemary.   Serves 6 to 8.

Serve with Korbel Champagne Cellars Chardonnay Champagne.

Recipe by Chef Robin Lehnhoff for
Korbel Champagne Cellars

Gorgonzola Cheese Balls

1 cup shelled walnut pieces
1 pound Gorgonzola
1 lemon; include zest and juice
2 teaspoons fresh thyme, chopped
3 tablespoons seasoned olive oil (such as
  sun-dried tomato or herb)
Salt and pepper to taste

Toast walnut pieces for 5 minutes, cool, and chop very fine.

Mix together cheese, lemon juice and zest, thyme, olive oil, salt and pepper. Blend well.

Pinch off 1-inch pieces of cheese mixture and roll in chopped walnuts to make balls. Chill.

Makes 25 portions.

Serve with Pezzi King Vineyards Zinfandel.

Lois Weinstein for
Pezzi King Vineyards

Jimtown's Romesco Sauce

This is Jimtown's version of the classic Spanish sauce, for Russian River Wine Road.

1 cup fine, fresh bread crumbs
1 cup whole, unblanched almonds
1/2 teaspoon crushed red pepper
2 garlic cloves, peeled and minced
3 cups plum tomatoes, seeded and chopped
2 medium sweet red peppers, roasted, peeled and chopped
6 tablespoons red wine vinegar
1/2 teaspoon sweet paprika
1/2 teaspoon salt
1/2 teaspoon freshly ground black pepper
1 cup extra virgin olive oil
1/2 teaspoon fresh lemon juice
1/2 teaspoon sugar

Preheat oven to 400 degrees. In a cake tin, toast the crumbs, stirring once or twice, until golden brown, about 15 minutes. Cool.

In a food processor, combine the crumbs, almonds, crushed red pepper and garlic. Process until the almonds are fairly evenly chopped. Add the tomatoes, peppers, vinegar, paprika, salt and pepper and process briefly.

With the motor running, gradually add the oil through the feed tube, stopping once to scrape down the sides; the sauce will thicken. Add the lemon juice and sugar and process to blend.

Place in a crock or bowl and serve as a dip.

We recommend this as a very tasty dip for grilled whiskey fennel sausage or any of your other favorite grilled sausages.

Serve with 1997 Field Stone Sangiovese or 1998 Field Stone Gewürztraminer.

Field Stone Winery and Vineyard

Shiitake Mushroom Tapenade

1-3/4 pounds shiitake mushrooms (caps only)
1/2 cup canola oil
1/4 cup garlic, minced
1 tablespoon fresh ginger, finely chopped
1/2 tablespoon chile garlic paste (Lan Chi brand)
1/4 cup soy sauce
3/4 cup sherry wine
1/4 cup sesame oil

Dice mushroom caps into 1/3" pieces. Sauté in 1/4 cup canola oil. Add rest of ingredients above. Mix well.

Mix together separately:
3/4 cup yellow onion, minced
1-1/4 cups canola oil
1/2 cup sesame oil
3/4 teaspoon salt
3/4 teaspoon pepper
1 tablespoon garlic, minced
1-3/4 teaspoons fresh ginger, chopped
1/2 cup rice vinegar
1/4 cup lemon juice

Mix well and add to mixture sautéing above. Heat to boil. Serve on sliced baguettes or toast points.

Makes 1 quart.

Serve with Belvedere Russian River Chardonnay.

Belvedere Vineyards & Winery and Tasting on the Plaza

SALADS

Crunchy Salad

2 cups green cabbage, shredded
2 cups purple cabbage, shredded
1 cup Granny Smith apples, cubed
1/4 cup golden raisins
1/4 cup chopped peanuts
1 cup sour cream or plain yogurt
2 tablespoons honey
2 tablespoons white wine vinegar
1 teaspoon aniseed
1 teaspoon caraway seeds
1/2 teaspoon ground white pepper
1/2 teaspoon garlic powder
Salt to taste

In a large bowl, mix honey, vinegar, pepper, garlic powder, aniseed and caraway seeds. Stir in sour cream or yogurt and gently fold in raisins, apples, peanuts and cabbage.

Serves 8.

Serve with Everett Ridge Russian River Chardonnay.

Everett Ridge Vineyards and Winery

Pear and Goat Cheese Salad

4 pieces dried pears, diced into 1/4-inch pieces
4 strips thin sliced bacon, diced into 1/4-inch pieces
2 cloves garlic, minced
4 ounces Sauvignon Blanc
4-1/2 ounces Laura Chenel Cabecou Cheese
   (reserving oil)
1 tablespoon balsamic vinegar
1 teaspoon Dijon mustard
2 teaspoons fresh thyme
1 tablespoon lemon juice
1 teaspoon lemon zest, minced
1/4 cup reserved oil marinade from Cabecou
4 cups mixed salad greens

At least 4 hours (or overnight) before assembling, place diced dried pears in bowl and add 2 ounces of Sauvignon Blanc to soak.

In medium skillet over medium heat, cook bacon until fat is rendered and bacon is cooked but not crisp. Drain and save bacon, discarding fat. In same skillet, over medium heat, add reserved marinade and scrape up bits. Add garlic and cook until soft, 4 to 6 minutes, then add bacon pieces. Reduce heat and add remaining Sauvignon Blanc, pears (with any remaining wine), mustard, lemon juice, lemon zest, thyme, vinegar and mix together.

Stir in half of the goat cheese, crumbled, and while warm, pour into large bowl over greens and toss. Crumble remaining goat cheese on top and serve.

Serves 4.

Serve with Alderbrook Dry Creek Sauvignon Blanc.

<u>*Tasting Notes:*</u>
This salad does a wonderful job of complementing all of the elements of the wine. It actually heightens complexity and components that one wouldn't usually find this early in the wine's development. The upfront pear in the nose of the wine, with just a hint of smokey vanilla, is enhanced by the dried, concentrated pear in the salad.

The bacon has a smoky richness which often may overwhelm other SVBL, but the richness of the mouthfeel and the crispness of the finish both harmonize the flavors and subtly define the components. Goat cheese is mildly tart and nutty while exhibiting a creamy texture. The cheese mirrors similar components in the wine, especially the creamy mouthfeel and wonderful lingering finish.

<u>*Herbs:*</u> *The mild but distinctive character comes with the addition of the fresh herbs and cheese marinade (if used). Here at the winery, I grow lemon thyme, which complements it well. In lieu of the lemon thyme, we use lemon zest, which heightens the citrus quality in the wine.*

Recipe created by Winery Chef Jim May for
Alderbrook Vineyards & Winery

Peruvian Purple Potato Salad

2 pounds purple potatoes
2 stalks celery, diced
1/4 cup fresh parsley, minced
1 cup mayonnaise
1/2 cup stone ground mustard with fresh
  horseradish
1/4 cup slivered almonds, toasted
Salt and pepper to taste
3 hard-boiled eggs, sliced

Bring potatoes to a boil in salted water. Reduce heat and simmer until potatoes are fork-tender. Drain; cut into bite-sized pieces. Toss with celery, mayonnaise, mustard, and parsley. Top with sliced eggs and slivered almonds. Serve at room temperature or cold.

Serves 10.

Serve with Taft Street Sauvignon Blanc.

Taft Street Winery

Spinach-Strawberry Salad with Goat Cheese Bruschetta

1/2 cup sugar
2 tablespoons sherry or white wine vinegar
1-1/2 teaspoons sesame seeds, toasted
1-1/2 teaspoons olive oil
1 teaspoon red onion, minced
3/4 teaspoon poppy seeds
1/4 teaspoon Hungarian sweet paprika
1/8 teaspoon salt
6 cups cleaned and torn spinach (about 1 pound)
2 cups halved strawberries
2 tablespoons slivered almonds, toasted
1 3-ounce log goat cheese, cut into 6 slices
6 slices French bread, toasted

Combine first 8 ingredients; cover. Mix thoroughly. Put aside.

Combine spinach and strawberries in a bowl; toss gently. Pour dressing over spinach mixture and toss gently again. Spoon salad onto plate; sprinkle each serving with 1 teaspoon almonds.

Spread cheese over toast to make your goat cheese bruschettas. Serve each salad with one bruschetta.

Serves 6.

Serve with 1997 Sebastopol Vineyards Dutton Ranch Chardonnay.

Sebastopol Vineyards

Tuscan Orzo Pasta

1 pound orzo pasta
1 tablespoon fresh garlic, chopped
1 cup golden raisins
1 cup toasted walnuts
1 bunch fresh basil, chopped
2 tablespoons white Balsamic vinegar
2 oranges, juice and zest
2 lemons, juice and zest
Salt and pepper to taste
1 cup tangerine oil

Cook orzo al dente according to package instructions. Set aside.

Toss raisins, walnuts, garlic, basil, juices, zests, and vinegar with pasta. Drizzle tangerine oil over all. Season with salt and pepper.

Serves 6 to 8.

Serve with Lake Sonoma Winery Chardonnay.

Recipe by Chef Robin Lehnhoff of
Korbel Delicatessen & Market
for

Lake Sonoma Winery

Lentil Salad with Mint Marinated Feta Cheese

2 tablespoons pine nuts, toasted
2 tablespoons fresh mint leaves
1 tablespoon fresh parsley, minced
6 cloves garlic, minced
1/4 cup + 3 tablespoons olive oil
4 ounces feta cheese, diced into 1/2-inch cubes
2 cups green lentils, cooked
2 carrots, diced in 1/2-inch cubes
2 leeks, sliced in thin slices
2 teaspoon cumin
1 teaspoon coriander
1/4 cup vinegar
1 teaspoon fresh ginger, minced

In a bowl, combine chopped mint, parsley, 3 cloves garlic, 2 tablespoon olive oil; season with pepper. Add feta cheese. Marinate 2 hours or overnight.

In a skillet, heat 1 tablespoon oil. Add carrots, leeks, remaining garlic and sauté until tender. Grind cumin and coriander together; add to pan with ginger. Sauté 3 minutes, add lentils and cook until warm. Whisk vinegar and remaining oil, toss with lentils. Season with salt and pepper. Garnish with feta mix and pine nuts.

Serves 8.

Serve with Blackstone '97 Chardonnay California or Martin Ray '97 Chardonnay California.

Blackstone Winery

ENTREES

Dry Creek Coq Au Zin

4 slices Applewood smoked bacon
4 large, boneless chicken breasts, with skin
1-1/2 cups yellow onion, diced medium
3 tablespoons all-purpose flour
1-1/2 cups chicken stock
1 cup Zinfandel
1 cup pitted prunes
1 teaspoon dried thyme

Fry bacon in sauté pan until brown and crisp. Put on paper towels and drain. Season chicken with salt and pepper and sauté in same pan until just cooked through, about 6 minutes per side. Transfer chicken to a plate.

Add onions to pan and sauté until starting to brown. Pour off all but 3 tablespoons of fat. Stir in flour and cook, stirring for 4 to 5 minutes. Add stock, wine, prunes, and thyme. Cover pan and simmer about 8 to 10 minutes. Uncover and increase heat and boil until sauce thickens, about 10 minutes more.

Return chicken to pan with any juices and heat through for 2 minutes. Serve on a platter with sauce and top with crumbled bacon bits.

Serves 4.

Serve with Alderbrook OVOC Zinfandel.

Alderbrook Winery

Gazpacho

5 pounds ripe tomatoes
2 medium-sized cucumbers (one whole for juicing; one peeled and seeded)
1/2 red onion
1 Serrano chile
1/2 bunch fresh basil, chopped
1/4 cup fresh parsley leaves
1 small jicama
6 stalks celery
2 teaspoons lime juice
Tabasco
2 teaspoons champagne vinegar
Salt and pepper

In a juicer or food processor, place 3 pounds of tomatoes, one whole cucumber, 1/4 red onion, 1/2 Serrano chile, 4 stalks of celery, and 1/4 cup parsley leaves. Process all ingredients on high speed; set aside.

Blanch tomatoes in boiling water, 10 seconds. Remove, chill and peel. Dice to medium-sized pieces. Fine dice remaining ingredients and add to reserved vegetable juice, along with the chopped tomatoes. Add chopped basil. Season with lime juice, vinegar, salt, pepper, and Tabasco. Chill for 1 hour before serving. Garnish with chopped basil.

Serves 8.

Serve with Kendall-Jackson 1997 Vintner's Reserve Sauvignon Blanc.

Prepared by Chefs Tess McDonough and Ed Walsh
Kendall-Jackson Wine Center

Plantation Pork

A colorful, hearty and festive dish.

2-1/2 pound pork butt, cubed and sautéed

SAUCE
2 tablespoons butter
1/4 cup flour
2-1/2 cups beef broth
1/3 cup chili sauce
1/3 cup onions, diced
1/4 cup tomato paste
Salt and pepper to taste
1 tablespoon molasses
1/2 cup Everett Ridge Old Vine Zinfandel
2 tablespoons brown sugar
1/3 cup apple cider vinegar
1/4 cup soy sauce
1/2 teaspoon garlic powder
1/2 teaspoon ginger
1/2 teaspoon thyme

Sauce: Melt butter and add flour to make a roux. Add remaining ingredients. Bring to slow boil and simmer 45 minutes.

To Serve: Add sautéed pork cubes. Serve with polenta or rice pilaf and grilled vegetables (peppers, mushrooms,zucchini, Japanese eggplant).

Serves 6.

Serve with Everett Ridge Old Vine Zinfandel or Everett Ridge Syrah.

Everett Ridge Winery

Prawns in Garlic and Wine

1 pound large prawns, 20 to 25 per pound
4 tablespoons olive oil
2 tablespoons flour
3 cloves garlic (or more)
1 tablespoon shallots
Pinch of salt
1/4 cup white wine
2 tablespoons butter
Lemon juice (ream 1/2 lemon)

Heat skillet, add olive oil and shallots. Mix flour and salt and coat shrimp in flour. Add shrimp and garlic to skillet and sauté for two or three minutes. Add white wine, butter and lemon juice. Serve with pasta and salad or as a side dish.

Serves 6.

Serve with Chardonnay.

Radio Station KSRO

Focaccia topped with Italian Sausage, Red Bell Peppers and Garlic Jack Cheese

1-1/2 loaves Bridgeford Bread Dough (or your
   favorite prepared yeast dough)
4 tablespoons cornmeal
12 ounces prepared pesto sauce
4 tablespoons olive oil
3/4 pound bulk Italian sausage
1/2 pound red bell peppers
1 large onion, diced
3/4 pound Garlic Jack cheese, grated
6 cloves garlic, minced
1 tablespoon coarsely ground black pepper
1 tablespoon fennel seeds
1 tablespoon salt

Form bread dough into a 12 x 17-inch sheet pan and sprinkle with cornmeal. Add 2 tablespoons of olive oil to pesto and brush onto dough.

Sauté all other ingredients together with rest of olive oil; drain off excess liquid. Mix thoroughly and spread over dough. Sprinkle cheese on top.

Bake at 375 degrees for 20 minutes, or until dough is baked and not too soft. Cool and serve. If prepared ahead and refrigerated, heat before serving.

Makes 24 portions.

Serve with Hop Kiln Winery's 1996 Zinfandel.

Hop Kiln Winery

Barbecued Ribs in Peanut Chipotle Sauce with Corn-Tomatillo Salsa

1 cup soy sauce
4 tablespoons fresh ginger, coarsely chopped
2 cups Optima Cabernet Sauvignon wine
2 racks of pork ribs (12 ribs each)
2-1/2 cups peanut-chipotle sauce (see below)
4 cups corn-tomatillo salsa (see below)
2 cups chopped peanuts

Preheat oven to 400 degrees.

In a saucepan over medium-high heat, combine the soy sauce, wine, and the ginger; bring to a boil. Pour mixture into the bottom of a roasting pan and place the ribs on a rack in the pan. Brush with the peanut-chipotle sauce.

Place in the oven and bake for 1-1/4 hours, basting every 10 minutes. Remove from oven and cut into single ribs. Stack or arrange ribs on plates, accompanied by the salsa. Just before serving, sprinkle with peanuts.

Peanut-Chipotle Sauce

1-1/2 cups barbecue sauce
1/2 cup smooth peanut butter
1/4 cup soy sauce
1-1/2 tablespoons rice wine vinegar
1-1/2 teaspoons puréed canned chipotles
1-1/2 tablespoons honey

Combine and mix well. Put aside.

Corn-Tomatillo Salsa

1 cup corn kernels
2 medium tomatillos, husked and chopped
1 tablespoon red onion, minced
1-1/2 teaspoons Jalapeño pepper, minced
2 tablespoons fresh lime juice
2 tablespoons fresh cilantro, chopped
1/2 teaspoon honey
Salt and pepper

Combine all ingredients. Season with salt and pepper.

These Barbecued Ribs are delicious cooked with the hot Peanut Chipotle Sauce and served with the fresh, crispy Corn-Tomatillo Salsa.

Serves 4.

Serve with Optima 1996 Cabernet Sauvignon.

Optima Wine Cellars

Lamb with Port Wine Sauce

1 boneless leg of lamb (3 to 4 pounds), bones
    reserved
4 cloves garlic, peeled
8 to 9 cloves garlic, slivered
3 cloves garlic, peeled and mashed
1-1/2 teaspoons rosemary
Pinch of nutmeg
1/4 teaspoon salt
1/4 teaspoon black pepper
1/4 cup olive oil
1 onion, sliced
2 carrots, peeled and sliced
1/2 teaspoon black peppercorns
3 whole cloves
1 bay leaf
6 cups Port
1/4 cup additional olive oil
1 stick butter
1/2 cup cassis (blackcurrant liqueur)

Trim excess fat from leg, rub inside and out with
garlic, then stuff with the garlic, rosemary, nutmeg.
Salt and pepper leg. With string, truss the leg back to
original shape. With a sharp knife, put slices in leg and
stuff with slivered garlic. In a large container, place
bones and lamb, cover with olive oil, onions, carrots,
rest of slivered garlic, peppercorns, cloves, bay leaf
and port. Marinate leg for two days.

Heat oven to 450 degrees. Remove leg from marinade and place in roasting pan. Place in oven. Reduce heat to 350 degrees immediately.

Roast for 1-1/4 to 1-3/4 hours, or until an instant meat thermometer reads 130 degrees for rare, or 140 degrees for medium-rare.

Sauce: Strain vegetables and bones from marinade. Reserve both. In large saucepan, heat the additional olive oil, pat bones dry, add the bones and sauté until brown. Add vegetables and cook until lightly browned.

Add the marinade, simmer until reduced to 2 cups. Skim occasionally to remove foam as it comes to the top. Strain, combine strained sauce and the cassis and reduce until it thickens to a light syrup. Incorporate the butter by bits with a whisk. Season to taste.

Serve with a Merlot or Cabernet Sauvignon.

Radio Station KMGG

Pork Tenderloin Sandwiches with Pinot Noir Sauce

4 tablespoons butter
2 whole pork tenderloins (about 2 pounds)
1/2 cup Kowzlowski Farms raspberry jam
2 tablespoons lemon juice
1/4 cup Sebastopol Vineyards "Dutton Ranch"
  Pinot Noir
Bread

Preheat oven to 350 degrees.

Melt 2 tablespoons butter in a large skillet. Add pork and brown on all sides. Remove to a baking pan.

Melt remaining butter in a saucepan. Add raspberry jam, lemon juice and wine. Blend well. Bring to boil and simmer for 5 to 7 minutes. Pour sauce over pork.

Roast for 30 minutes, basting often until meat reaches 160 degrees when tested with a meat thermometer inserted in the center of the tenderloin.

Slice pork and serve on your favorite sandwich bread with any additional pinot-raspberry sauce drizzled over pork.

Serves 8 to 10.

Serve with 1997 Sebastopol Vineyards "Dutton Ranch" Pinot Noir.

Sebastopol Vineyards

Penne Pasta with Red Peppers and Garlic

8 ounces (1/2 package) dry penne pasta
4 medium red peppers (core removed), sliced in
  small, fine strips
8 cloves garlic, minced
6 tablespoons virgin olive oil
1 cup dry white wine
1 cup homemade chicken broth
Juice of 1 lemon
Salt and pepper to taste

Cook pasta according to package directions. Drain and put aside, keeping warm.

Sauté peppers and garlic in olive oil over low heat until softened, 10 to 12 minutes, stirring often. Add 1 teaspoon salt. Add wine and raise heat, cooking until wine is reduced. Add chicken stock and reduce again until peppers are glazed. Season with salt, pepper and lemon.

Combine sauce and pasta. Toss gently. Serve.

Serves 4.

Serve with Sausal Private Reserve Zinfandel.

Sausal Winery

Mill Creek Vineyard's Italian Heritage Lasagna

1-1/2 pounds good quality ground beef
1/2 pound bulk ground Italian Sausage
1 very large onion, or two medium onions, minced
4 cloves garlic, minced
2 green peppers, diced (if desired)
1-1/2 tablespoons Italian seasoning (or fresh Italian
   herbs)
1/4 pound Ricotta cheese
1 pound Parmesan cheese, grated
1 12 to 14-ounce can tomato paste, or 2 6-ounce cans
1 14-ounce can tomato sauce
2 <u>heaping</u> cups tomatoes, chopped
1 cup red wine (Merlot, Cabernet or Zinfandel)
Salt and pepper to taste
1 box lasagna noodles
1 pound Mozzarella cheese, grated
Tomato juice to moisten

Brown meats. Brown onions, garlic, and green pepper. Combine with the tomato sauce, paste, tomatoes, wine, and seasoning. Simmer for at least 1 hour.

Cook lasagna noodles according to package instructions.

Assembly:
Place 3 cooked lasagna noodles in bottom of a 13x9x2-inch baking pan. Spread with meat mixture, then Ricotta, then Parmesan, then Mozzarella cheeses. Continue layering. Top with a layer of noodles. Top with Parmesan cheese. Add tomato juice to moisten.

Assembly:
Bake 45 minutes to 1 hour at 350 degrees until hot and bubbly throughout. Add additional tomato juice if top becomes too dry.

Serves 8.

Serve with Mill Creek Vineyards Estate Dry Creek Valley Merlot.

Mill Creek Vineyards

Pork Fumé Verde

12 ounces heavy cream
3 heaping tablespoons fresh tarragon, minced
3 tablespoons olive oil
2 tablespoons unsalted butter
3 shallots, thinly sliced
1-1/2 pounds pork loin, cut into 3/4-inch cubes
3/4 pound mushrooms, quartered
1 tablespoon roasted garlic purée
1/2 teaspoon salt
1/2 teaspoon white pepper
4 tablespoons lemon juice
1 tablespoon lemon zest, finely minced
1/2 cup fresh parsley, minced
1 medium carrot, shredded
1 pound Bowtie pasta
1/2 cup Dry Creek Vineyard Reserve Fumé Blanc

In a heavy-bottomed saucepan, bring cream to a boil and reduce by half. Add 2 heaping tablespoons of tarragon to cream. Set aside.

In a sauté pan, using oil and butter, sauté shallots and pork over high heat for about 5 minutes. Add mushrooms, garlic, salt and pepper. Cook until mushrooms start giving up liquid.

Remove from heat and strain all liquid into a small saucepan; add the wine, lemon juice, and lemon zest, and reduce down to almost a syrup. Stir reduced liquid into the cream mixture and add remaining tablespoon of tarragon and parsley. Stir into pork mixture and simmer over low heat for 10 minutes.

Prepare Bowtie pasta according to package directions. Drain pasta then add to pork mixture. Garnish with the grated carrot and additional parsley. Serve with a steamed vegetable sourdough bread.

Serves 4.

Serve with a Dry Creek Vineyard Reserve Fumé Blanc.

Recipe by Richard Nollevaux for
Dry Creek Vineyard

Smoked Salmon and Corn Chowder

6 ounces bacon, diced
1/2 cup butter
2 onions, chopped
2 stalks celery, chopped
2 cloves garlic, minced
1 teaspoon paprika
1 teaspoon tarragon
3 tablespoons all-purpose flour
7 cups milk
4-1/2 cups potatoes, diced into 1/4-inch pieces
2 cups corn
8 ounces smoked salmon, chopped
2 teaspoons freshly squeezed lemon juice
2 teaspoons freshly ground black pepper
2 teaspoons salt

In a large pot, sauté bacon over medium heat until crisp. Pour out excess fat. Add butter and increase heat to medium-high. Add onions, celery, and garlic; sauté until tender. Add paprika and tarragon. Sprinkle flour over onion mixture and stir with a whisk until flour is absorbed. Slowly whisk in 1 cup of the milk until blended. Whisk in remaining milk. Stir in potatoes, corn, smoked salmon, lemon juice, pepper, and salt. Stirring constantly, bring chowder just to a boil, then reduce heat to low and simmer until potatoes are tender and chowder is thick.

Serves 8.

Serve with Geyser Peak 1996 Reserve Chardonnay.

Geyser Peak Winery

Spaghetti with Gorgonzola and Macadamia Nuts

With a salad of wild greens and pears, this creamy pasta dish would be a perfect light supper.

2 tablespoons butter
2 cloves garlic, crushed
4 ounces Gorgonzola, crumbled
1/4 cup sour cream
3/4 cup Mauna Loa macadamia nuts, finely chopped
Salt and freshly ground white pepper
12 ounces spaghetti

In a large saucepan, melt butter over medium heat. Add garlic and sauté until fragrant. Add the crumbled Gorgonzola and stir until melted. Add sour cream and stir to make a creamy sauce. Stir in the macadamia nuts. Season with salt and pepper to taste.

Cook the spaghetti in boiling, salted water according to package instructions. Drain the spaghetti well, then add to the sauce in the pan. Stir gently until coated and serve immediately.

Serves 4.

Serve with Canyon Road Venezia Chardonnay.

Canyon Road Winery

Pasta Salad with Chicken and Sun-Dried Tomato Pesto

1 pound breast of chicken, boned and skinned
2 large green squash
2 large yellow squash
2 pounds shell pasta, small to medium size

SUN DRIED TOMATO PESTO
2 cups sun-dried tomatoes
1 cup Chateau Souverain Zinfandel
1/2 cup Parmesan cheese
3 tablespoons fresh parsley, chopped
Lime juice
1 tablespoon black pepper
2 tablespoons garlic, chopped
1-1/2 cups olive oil

Grill the chicken, season lightly, and cool in the refrigerator for one hour.Slice the squash lengthwise, brush lightly with oil and grill until tender. Set aside to cool.

Cook pasta 8 to 10 minutes, drain and place in cold water, then drain once again. Refrigerate.

Place tomatoes and Zinfandel in a saucepan and bring to a boil; turn off the heat and let the mixture sit for 10 minutes.

In a food processor, add tomato mixture and pulse until well combined. Add all other ingredients except oil. Pulse again. With processor on, slowly drop in the olive oil until combined.

Chop the chicken and squash into bite-sized pieces and fold together the chicken, squash, pesto and pasta. Season to taste and garnish with Italian parsley.

Serves 8.

Serve with Chateau Souverain Zinfandel.

Martin Courtman, Executive Chef
Chateau Souverain

Salmon with Red Thai Curry Sauce

4 salmon filets, 5 ounces each, grilled
1 cup coconut milk
1/4 cup Thai basil*
1/4 cup bell pepper, finely sliced
2 tablespoons red curry paste (see below)
2 tablespoons krachai (a ginger-like root)*
1 tablespoon coriander seed, pounded
1 tablespoon soy or fish sauce
1 tablespoon sugar
1 teaspoon cumin seed, roasted and pounded
2 kaffir lime leaves, chopped*

Red Thai Curry Paste
Prepare this curry paste in advance.

5 large chili peppers, opened and soaked in warm
    water for 15 minutes
1/4 cup lemon grass, sliced*
1 to 2 tablespoons shallots, chopped
1-1/2 teaspoons coriander root, chopped*
1/2 teaspoon kaffir lime peel (Thai lime), chopped*
1/2 teaspoon galanga (a ginger-like root), sliced*
1/2 teaspoon shrimp paste
1/2 teaspoon salt

Pound all curry paste ingredients together into paste
consistency. Put aside.

*All ingredients marked with asterisks may be found
at Asian markets.*

To prepare Red Thai Curry Sauce, boil one-half of the coconut milk in a wok until you see the coconut oil rise to the surface. Blend in the curry paste and cook until the fragrance begins to rise. Add the coriander, cumin, and kaffir lime leaves. Add the remaining coconut milk, krachai, fish or soy sauce, sugar, basil, and bell pepper. Cook until heated through and well blended.

Serve your hot Grilled Salmon Filets topped with sauce.

Serves 4.

You will enjoy this with Davis Bynum Pinot Noir.

As prepared by Chef Nit Bynum
Davis Bynum Winery

Spicy Calamari Vinaigrette with Sommer Vineyard Salsa

1 medium green bell pepper, julienned
1 medium red bell pepper, julienned
1 cup Spanish olives with pimientos, sliced
1/2 cup capers
1 medium red onion, sliced
1 tablespoon whole grain mustard
1/4 cup olive oil
1/4 cup red wine vinegar
1 teaspoon fresh ground black pepper
1 teaspoon salt
3 pounds calamari, tubes and tentacles cleaned
12 tortillas

Lightly poach the calamari for a few minutes. Drain. Cut tubes into thin rings, tentacle into pieces, and mix with all other ingredients. Set aside. Refrigerate.

In the meantime, prepare the Sommer Vineyard Salsa.

SOMMER VINEYARD SALSA
1 medium head of cabbage
3 tomatoes, chopped
4 Jalapeño peppers, seeded and chopped
2 medium onions, chopped
3 tablespoons olive oil
4 limes, juiced
3 ounces tequila
Salt and pepper to taste

In food processor, shred cabbage very thin. Put into mixing bowl. Chop onions and jalapeños coarsely. Add chopped tomatoes. Put in bowl with cabbage and mix. Add olive oil, lime juice, and tequila. Salt and pepper to taste. Mix. Set aside for 1 hour. Retaste and adjust seasonings.

To Serve:
Warm 12 tortillas on a grill. Spoon salsa on tortillas. Top with calamari. Roll and eat.

Serves 12.

Serve with 1997 Sommer Vineyard Chardonnay or 1997 Sommer Vineyard Sangiovese.

Sommer Vineyards & Winery

Pork Loin with "Wild Boar Marinade" in a Roasted Mustard Crust

ROAST MARINADE
2 tablespoons olive oil
3 medium carrots, chopped
1 large onion, chopped
2 large shallots, chopped
3 medium garlic cloves, minced
5 cups Mark West Pinot Noir
1/2 cup red wine vinegar
4 medium bay leaves
6 parsley stalks, roughly chopped
16 juniper berries
2 teaspoons salt
12 black peppercorns

5 to 6 pound boneless, center-cut loin of pork, trimmed

MUSTARD CRUST
3 large garlic cloves, roughly chopped
1/3 cup scallions, coarsely chopped
1/4 cup dry white wine
1 teaspoon herbs d'Provence
1 cup old-fashioned mustard
1/4 cup olive oil
1/2 teaspoon freshly ground black pepper
2 teaspoon olive oil

Make the marinade:

Heat the oil over medium heat and cook vegetables until lightly browned. Add the wine, vinegar, and seasonings, then bring to a boil. Simmer for 10 minutes and allow to cool. Place meat in glass dish, cover with marinade and cover with plastic wrap. Refrigerate for 2 to 3 days, turning once or twice.

Make the crust:

In a food processor, quickly process the garlic, scallions, wine, and herbs until smooth. Add the remaining ingredients and process just until blended.

Preheat oven to 400 degrees. Remove pork from marinade, pat dry. In a large skillet, sear pork on all sides until lightly brown. Place on rack in baking pan and coat with mustard mixture. Roast until just done (about 30 minutes, or until internal temperature reaches 160 degrees). Allow to rest 5 minutes before serving.

Serves 12.

Serve with Mark West Russian River Valley Pinot Noir.

Mark West Estate Winery

Greens and Olive Salad with Southwest-Style Flank Steak

Marinated and grilled flank steak tossed with baby spinach, arugula and baby greens mixed with a currant and fig balsamic dressing, olive tapenade and croutons.

3 pounds flank steak

MARINADE
3 teaspoons fresh oregano, finely chopped
3 teaspoons fresh rosemary, finely chopped
3 teaspoons fresh sage, finely chopped
2 teaspoons garlic, finely chopped
2 teaspoons hot paprika
2 teaspoons curry powder
2 teaspoons Molido brand chile powder
2 cups apple cider or apple juice
1/2 cup lemon juice

SALAD GREENS
1 pound baby spinach
1 pound baby arugula
1 pound baby greens

DRESSING
1 cup olive oil
1/4 cup currant balsamic vinegar
1/4 cup fig balsamic vinegar
Salt and pepper to taste

TAPENADE
1/2 cup Kalamata olives
1/4 cup olive oil

CROUTONS
Slice one baguette into 1-inch squares. Bake in the oven until toasted.

Marinate flank steak with the seasonings, apple juice and lemon juice for three days. Grill and thinly slice the flank steak.

Grind olives and oil in Cuisinart until fine.

Make croutons by slicing a baguette loaf, then cut into 1-inch squares. Bake in oven until toasted. Toss the croutons with the tapenade mixture once they are cool.

Toss greens with dressing, add flank steak and tapenade/croutons mixture. Serve at room temperature.

Serves 20.

Serve with Rodney Strong Sonoma County Merlot.

Rodney Strong Vineyards

Rosato Risotto

A De Natale Family favorite.

1 medium onion, diced
2 tablespoons olive oil
8 cloves garlic, minced
3 cups chicken broth
1 cup jasmine rice
4 Roma tomatoes, diced
1/2 cup De Natale Rosato
2 cooked and diced turkey sausages
1/2 cup Romano cheese, grated

Sauté first three ingredients in a 3-quart saucepan until onion is limp. Add broth and rice to saucepan, cover and let simmer over low heat until most of the broth is absorbed, approximately 10 minutes.

Add the last four ingredients to rice and let simmer until rice is tender.

Serves 6.

Serve with :
1997 De Natale Estate Russian River Valley Rosato
or
1996 De Natale Estate Russian River Valley Pinot Noir.

De Natale Vineyards

Hanna Lamb Curry

2 pounds lamb stew meat, diced
1/4 cup olive oil
1 yellow onion, diced
4 cloves garlic, chopped
2 cups Hanna Chardonnay
2 cups tart apples, diced
1/2 cup raisins
1 20-ounce can pineapple chunks
3 heaping tablespoons curry powder
1/2 pint heavy cream
2 tablespoons cornstarch
Salt and pepper to taste
8 servings of steamed rice
1/4 cup toasted coconut

In a heavy gauge saucepan, sear the lamb in olive oil at high heat, adding the onions and garlic as the meat begins to brown. Add Hanna Chardonnay; continue to cook for approximately 30 minutes at medium heat, stirring occasionally. Add the fruit and curry powder and continue to cook for an additional 20 minutes. Add the cream. Season to taste. Thicken with cornstarch if needed.

Serve over steamed rice with optional garnish of toasted coconut.

Serves 8.

Serve with Hanna Reserve Sauvignon Blanc or Hanna Pinot Noir.

Hanna Winery
Alexander Valley & Santa Rosa

Penne Pasta with Blue Cheese and Basil

1 pound penne pasta, cooked according to package
   directions
2 bunches fresh basil, chopped
1/2 cup olive oil
1/4 cup garlic, chopped
1 cup Danish blue cheese, crumbled
1/3 cup toasted pine nuts or walnuts (optional)

Toss penne pasta with olive oil and garlic. Stir in basil
and blue cheese. Add salt and pepper to taste. Garnish
with nuts and fresh basil sprigs.

Serves 8.

*Serve with Lambert Bridge 1996 Sonoma County
Merlot.*

Lambert Bridge Winery

DESSERTS

Mill Creek Merlot Dark Chocolate Cake

1-3/4 cups sugar
2 cups flour
1 cup unsweetened cocoa (like Hershey's)
1-1/2 teaspoons baking soda
1-1/2 teaspoons baking powder
1 teaspoon salt
2 eggs
1 cup buttermilk
1/3 cup vegetable oil

2/3 cup Merlot*
1/3 cup water*

***boiling hot when added**

Heat oven to 350 degrees. Spray a rectangular 13x9x2-inch pan with vegetable spray; dust lightly with flour.

In large mixer bowl, combine dry ingredients. Add eggs, buttermilk, and oil. Beat on medium speed for 2 minutes. In microwave, heat Merlot and water to boiling. Stir boiling mixture into dry ingredients with spoon until well mixed. Batter will be thin. Pour into prepared pan. Bake 35 to 40 minutes or until wooden pick inserted in center comes out clean. Dust with powdered sugar, if desired.

Serves 12 to 15.

Serve with Mill Creek Vineyards Dry Creek Valley Zinfandel.

Mill Creek Vineyards

Triple Chocolate Cappucino Brownies with Raspberry Port Glaze

BROWNIES
6 ounces (1-1/2 sticks) butter
4-1/2 ounces unsweetened chocolate, chopped
1 tablespoon instant espresso powder
1/2 teaspoon ground cinnamon
3 ounces bittersweet chocolate, coarsely chopped
1/2 cup toasted almonds, chopped
1-1/4 cups sugar
3 large eggs
3/4 cup all-purpose flour

Stir first four ingredients in a large heavy saucepan over low heat until smooth. Remove from heat. Add chopped bittersweet chocolate and nuts. Stir until blended then whisk in sugar and eggs. Stir in flour. Transfer to baking dish. Bake until tester inserted into center comes out with moist crumbs attached, about 30 minutes. Cool on rack. Make up to 8 hours ahead.

Make white chocolate sauce.

WHITE CHOCOLATE SAUCE
2/3 cup whipping cream
1/2 cup whole espresso coffee beans
5 ounces white chocolate, chopped
1/8 teaspoon ground nutmeg

Bring cream and espresso beans to simmer in heavy saucepan. Cover, remove from heat and let steep 30 minutes. Strain into small saucepan. Add chocolate, stir over low heat until smooth. Add nutmeg. Can be made in advance, but cover and chill. Before using, warm over low heat until just melted.

RASPBERRY GLAZE
1/2 cup port
1 tablespoon cornstarch
6 ounces raspberries, puréed and strained
2 tablespoons sugar

Whisk port and cornstarch together in a small saucepan. Heat to a simmer until mixture becomes very thick. Remove from heat and mix with raspberry purée and sugar. Whisk until smooth. Make in advance.

Assembly:
Using 2-1/2-inch cookie cutter, cut out rounds of chocolate brownies. Spoon white chocolate sauce on bottom of small plate. Place 1 brownie in center of each plate. Spoon raspberry glaze on top of brownies.

Serves 8.

Serve with Alderbrook Ruby Port.

Alderbrook Winery

Blackberry Crisp

**8 tablespoons butter, melted and cooled, plus
  butter for greasing the pan
2 packages frozen blackberries or other berries
3/4 cup granulated sugar
1 tablespoon cinnamon
1 teaspoon nutmeg
1 tablespoon vanilla
1-1/2 cups dark brown sugar
1/2 cup rolled oats
3/4 cup chopped pecans or walnuts
1-1/4 cups flour**

Preheat oven to 375 degrees. Butter generously a 3-quart rectangular or oval baking dish.

Combine granulated sugar and 1/2 cup of dark brown sugar, 1/4 cup of the flour, cinnamon, nutmeg, and vanilla with the defrosted blackberries. Place in prepared baking dish.

Using your hands, combine the remaining flour, brown sugar, oats, nuts, and melted butter. Sprinkle this topping over the blackberry mixture.

Bake for 35 to 40 minutes or until the blackberries are bubbling and the topping is crisp and browned. Remove from the oven and cool. Can be served with vanilla ice cream or sweetened whipped cream.

Serves 6 to 8.

Serve with a glass of Christopher Creek Petite Syrah.

Christopher Creek Winery

Zinfandel Port Chocolate Balls

1 12-ounce box vanilla wafers
1/2 cup Dutch-processed unsweetened cocoa
1 cup slivered almonds
1/4 cup dark corn syrup
1/2 cup Sommer Vineyards Zinfandel Port
1/2 cup powdered sugar

In food processor, combine vanilla wafers, unsweetened cocoa, and slivered almonds. Whirl until fine crumbs form. Add corn syrup and Zinfandel Port. Mix until blended. Form into 1-inch balls. Roll in powdered sugar. Refrigerate before serving.

Makes 48 balls.

Serve with Sommer Vineyard Zinfandel Port.

Sommer Vineyards & Winery

Caterina's Biscotti

6 eggs, beaten well
2-1/2 cups sugar
5 teaspoons baking powder
5 cups flour
3 teaspoons vanilla extract
3 teaspoons lemon extract
1/2 cup vegetable oil

Mix dry ingredients together. Put wet ingredients with dry and mix by hand with wooden spoon until you have a big ball of dough. Let stand overnight.

Take dough and form 2 to 3-inch loaves by rolling. Loaves will be 10 to 12 inches long. Place rolls on cookie sheet and bake at 350 degrees for 25 minutes. Take out and cut into diagonal slices. Put back into oven for 10 to 15 minutes. Check frequently so biscotti will not burn.

Makes 50 to 60 biscotti.

Serve with F. Teldeschi Late Harvest Muscat Zinfandel or F. Teldeschi Zinfandel Port.

F. Teldeschi Winery

Cherries, Cherries, Cherries

1 pound fresh cherries, pitted
1/2 pound bittersweet Belgian chocolate

Melt chocolate slowly over low heat in a small pan, stirring as it melts, or place chocolate in the top of a double boiler over simmering water. Remove the top of the double boiler when the chocolate is slightly more than half melted. Stir until smooth.

Dip the cherries in the melted chocolate. Place on platter to cool. Place in refrigerator for 5 minutes to cool and set. Serve cold.

Serves 6 to 8.

Serve with Rodney Strong Sonoma County Merlot.

Rodney Strong Vineyards

Chocolate Matrix Mousse Tarts

MOUSSE
1 pint cream
1-2/3 pounds semi-sweet chocolate
2/3 cup Mazzocco Matrix
2-2/3 cups sugar
8 egg whites
1 cup water
Pinch salt

SWEET PASTRY SHELL
2-1/4 cups flour
7 tablespoons butter
3/4 cup powdered sugar, sifted
Small pinch salt
2 large eggs at room temperature

Pastry Shells: Put flour on cutting board and make a well in the center. Cut butter into small pieces and place in center of well. Work with your fingertips until completely softened. Add sugar and salt; mix well. Add eggs and mix. Gradually draw flour from sides of well into mixture.

When all is mixed, knead with palm of hand 2 to 3 times more until dough is very smooth. Roll into ball, flatten slightly, and cover with plastic wrap. Refrigerate several hours. Roll out dough to 1/8-inch thick, and cut to fit tartlette shell. Bake until golden at 350 degrees.

<u>Mousse Filling</u>: In heavy-bottomed sauce pot, bring sugar and water to boil. Boil to soft ball stage (240 degrees) and set aside. In double boiler, melt chocolate with the Matrix wine over barely simmering water. Mix frequently until smooth and melted. Set aside.

In a mixer, beat egg whites with the pinch of salt. When egg whites form soft peaks, add the hot syrup in a slow, steady stream. Beat on medium speed for 20 minutes until egg whites are cool. In a separate bowl, beat cream to soft peaks.

For assembly, gently fold 1/3 of the egg whites into the cooled chocolate mixture. Continue folding egg whites in thirds, then gently fold the whipped cream in until all are homogenous. Spoon into tarts. Chill and serve.

Makes 50 to 60 tarts, depending on size.

Serve with Mazzocco Vineyards Matrix.

Recipe by Eager to Please Catering for
Mazzocco Vineyards

Raspberry-Pinot Noir Sorbet

1 cup water
2 pints fresh raspberries
2 tablespoons lemon juice
1-1/4 cups sugar
1/4 cup Optima Pinot Noir
1/4 cup light corn syrup

In a large saucepan, heat water and sugar to boiling. Add raspberries. Heat again. Transfer to food processor. Purée. Strain into large bowl, cover, and refrigerate 1 hour until cold.

Add lemon juice, wine and syrup into chilled purée. Freeze in an ice cream maker according to manufacturer's directions.

Makes 1 quart.

Serve with Optima Vineyard 1997 Russian River Pinot Noir.

Optima Wine Cellars

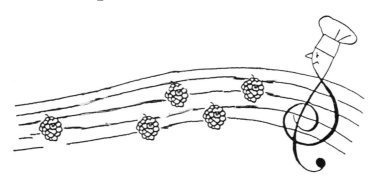

WINNING RECIPES
OF 1998

Gorgonzola Balls with Walnut Pesto

1-1/2 cups toasted walnut halves
Zest of 1 lemon, finely chopped
Juice of 1 lemon
2 teaspoons fresh thyme, chopped
1 clove garlic, crushed
1/4 teaspoon chili flakes
1/4 cup good quality olive oil, flavored with
   chili flakes
Salt and pepper to taste
1/2 pound Gorgonzola

Toast walnuts for about 5 minutes in a 350-degree oven. Allow walnuts to cool completely.

Chop walnuts finely. Do not use a food processor because it causes walnuts to become oily. Add lemon zest, juice, garlic, thyme and dipping oil to walnuts and combine well. Season to taste with salt and pepper.

Pinch off 1-inch pieces of gorgonzola and roll into balls. Roll balls in walnut pesto. Serve immediately.

Makes 16 pieces.

Chateau Souverain Merlot is recommended with this recipe.

Recipe by Martin Courtman, Executive Chef for
Chateau Souverain

Dry Creek's Zin Kickin' Chicken with Banjo Rice

4 boneless/skinless chicken breasts, cut into 1/2 to
   3/4-inch cubes
3 cups mushrooms, sliced
1/2 bell pepper, sliced 1-inch julienne
1 bunch green onions, thinly sliced (equal parts,
   white and green)
1 medium red onion, minced
3 cloves garlic, minced
3 tablespoons Rich's Rub (see recipe below)*
2 tablespoons butter
2 tablespoons olive oil
1/4 cup raspberry vinegar
1/2 cup Dry Creek Valley Zinfandel
1-1/2 cup chicken stock
3 tablespoons parsley, minced

BANJO RICE
1 cup rice (your favorite)
1 cup pineapple juice
1 cup chicken stock
1 teaspoon Rich's Rub* (see recipe below)
1 teaspoon salt
1 tablespoon (heaping) combination of orange,
   lemon, lime zest, finely minced

In a medium saucepan, bring pineapple juice and chicken stock to boil. Stir in rice, season with Rich's Rub, salt and zest. Reduce heat to low, cover and simmer for about 40 minutes until liquid is absorbed.

*RICH'S RUB
2 teaspoons salt
4 teaspoons paprika
1 teaspoon black pepper
1 teaspoon white pepper
1 teaspoon garlic powder
1 teaspoon onion powder
1 teaspoon dried oregano
1 teaspoon dried thyme
1 teaspoon chili powder
1/2 teaspoon cayenne pepper
1/2 teaspoon cumin

Combine all ingredients. *Recipe can be increased and stored for other uses. Use rub for ribs, tri-tips, or even grilled vegetables.*

Prepare chicken: Sprinkle chicken with 3 tablespoons Rich's Rub, put into covered container, and refrigerate 6 hours or overnight.

Use a large, heavy-bottomed pan. On high heat, sauté the onions and bell peppers in 2 tablespoons of oil for 5 minutes. Add garlic and chicken and cook for 5 minutes. Add mushrooms and cook for 5 minutes more. Add Zinfandel, raspberry vinegar and chicken stock. Bring to a boil, then reduce heat and simmer for 10 to 15 minutes, until flavors marry. Add parsley and serve over Banjo Rice.

Serves 4 to 6.

Serve with Dry Creek Valley Reserve Zinfandel or Dry Creek Valley Reserve Chardonnay.

Dry Creek Vineyard

Albóndigas al Ajillo

Meatballs in garlic sauce.

3 tablespoons olive oil
2 heads garlic, peeled and left whole
3 1-inch slices of French bread (in rounds)
1 pound ground beef
4 tablespoons fresh parsley, minced
1 teaspoon salt
1/2 teaspoon black pepper
1/4 teaspoon nutmeg
1 egg
1-1/2 cup beef or chicken stock
2 medium tomatoes
All-purpose flour for coating

Heat 2 tablespoons of olive oil in a skillet and add all but 3 or 4 cloves of the garlic. Sauté until golden and remove. Toast 1 slice of the bread in the remaining oil. Break up the toasted bread and food process together with the cooked garlic. Reserve.

In a shallow bowl, soak the remaining 2 bread slices in water to cover, then squeeze dry. Mince the remaining cloves of garlic and combine in a large bowl with the soaked bread, meat, 2 tablespoons of the parsley, salt, pepper, nutmeg, and egg. Work the mixture with your hands until well mixed. Form into cocktail-sized balls. Toss the meatballs with the flour into a shallow bowl to coat. Shake off the excess flour.

Heat the remaining tablespoon of oil in a large skillet, add the meatballs and cook over medium heat until browned on all sides. Pour the stock over the meatballs. Cut the tomatoes in half and, using a grater, hold a tomato half in your hand and grate directly into the skillet. Discard the skin. Stir in the reserved ground garlic-bread mixture. Cover and simmer for 30 minutes.

Sprinkle the remaining parsley over the meatballs and sauce and serve with toothpicks for tapas or serve with potatoes or pasta.

Serves 10 as an appetizer.

Serve with Forchini Vineyard 1997 Zinfandel Dry Creek Valley Estate Bottled.

Forchini Vineyards

Chevre Cheesecake with Biscotti Crust

CRUST
6 ounces soft butter
1-1/2 cup confectioner's sugar
2 cups all-purpose flour
1 cup biscotti crumbs
1/2 cup ground walnuts

FILLING
2 cups cream cheese, room temperature
1 cup goat cheese
4 eggs
1/2 cup sugar
1 tablespoon chopped rosemary
1 teaspoon salt

Preheat oven to 225 degrees. Place butter, confectioner's sugar, flour, walnuts and biscotti crumbs in a 5-quart mixing bowl with a paddle attachment. Beat on low speed until ingredients are incorporated. Do not cover mix.

Press the dough into pan, being careful to press the dough evenly on the bottom and sides of pan. Place pan in the refrigerator for 30 minutes to allow the dough to set. Place cream cheese and goat cheese in a 5-quart mixing bowl with paddle attachment and beat on low speed until incorporated. Add eggs one at a time until incorporated. Add sugar, rosemary, and salt. Mix for 1 minute.

Remove pan with the crust from refrigerator and pour the batter into the pan. Place in oven and bake for 2 minutes. Check for doneness with a toothpick or cake tester. The toothpick will be clean and the cheesecake will not be fluid. If the batter is still runny, turn the oven off and allow cake to remain in the oven until firm. Remove from oven and allow to cool.

Serves 12 to 16.

Serve with Kendall-Jackson Camelot Vineyards Chardonnay.

Kendall-Jackson Wine Center

Citrus Chicken Salad in Endive Leaves

6 chicken breasts, poached* (recipe for poaching
  liquid follows)
Zest and juice of 1 lime, zest minced
Zest and juice of 1 lemon, zest minced
1 cup mayonnaise
2 tablespoons olive oil
1 green apple, diced
1/2 cup dried cranberries
1/2 cup dried apricots, diced
1/2 cup celery, diced
1/2 cup green onions, thinly sliced
2 heads endive, leaves cleaned
Salt and pepper to taste

*POACHING LIQUID
2 cups cold water
1/2 cup Chardonnay
1/2 cup yellow onion, chopped
1/2 cup carrot, chopped
2 tablespoons juniper berries
1 bay leaf

In a medium saucepan, combine water, wine, onion, carrot, juniper berries, and bay leaf. Bring to boil and immediately turn heat down. Add chicken breasts and simmer gently for about 15 minutes, or until chicken is cooked through. Remove from poaching liquid and cool completely. Dice into 1-inch cubes.

In a small bowl, combine mayonnaise, lime zest and juice, and lemon zest and juice. Whisk olive oil into mayonnaise mixture. Salt and pepper to taste.

In a large bowl, combine diced chicken, apple, cranberries, apricots, celery and green onions. Dress with citrus mayonnaise. Check seasoning and add salt and pepper if needed.

Spoon 1 tablespoon of the chicken salad mixture onto endive leaves and serve immediately.

Serves 8 to 10.

Chateau Souverain Chardonnay pairs well with this recipe.

Martin Courtman, Executive Chef
Chateau Souverain

Wild Rice, Chicken and Walnut Salad

6 cups canned chicken broth
8 ounces wild rice, uncooked (1-1/2 cups)
2-1/2 pounds roasted chicken, skinned and boned,
   with meat cut into 1/3-inch pieces
1 red bell pepper, chopped
2 bunches arugula or spinach, chopped
1/4 cup green onions, chopped
3 tablespoons soy sauce
3 tablespoons rice vinegar
3 tablespoons Oriental sesame oil
2 cups walnuts, toasted and chopped
1 head of romaine lettuce

Bring chicken broth to a boil in a saucepan. Add rice and bring to a boil. Reduce heat to low, cover and cook until just tender, about 50 minutes. Drain well. Transfer rice to a large bowl. Mix in chicken, red bell pepper, arugula or spinach and green onions. Mix soy sauce, vinegar and oil in a small bowl. Pour over salad and mix. Season with salt and pepper. Mix in nuts. Arrange romaine leaves on platter around salad.

Serves 12.

Serve with Christopher Creek Syrah.

Christopher Creek Winery

WINE AND FOOD PAIRING

Wine & Food Pairing

Pairing wine and food should be fun and easy. It is almost as interesting to find out which wines and food do not complement each other as which do. Listed below are some basics of wine and food pairing, although the most important fact in any wine and food pairing is to enjoy the wine and food with family and friends.

Sauvignon Blanc, Fumé Blanc

Sauvignon Blanc and Fumé Blanc may range from very herbal or grassy to melon and citrus. It is usually fermented dry and develops as a medium-bodied wine.

	YES	*NO*
Seafood:	Most shellfish: raw or cooked and with light sauces	Lobster
Fish:	Poached, grilled or baked	Sturgeon
Meat:	Chicken, turkey	Sausage, foie gras
Cheese:	Goat and Parmesan	Brie, Swiss, Blue
Herbs & Spices:	Black pepper, capers, chives, Garlic, cumin, oregano, sage	Cinnamon, cloves Curry, ginger
Sauces:	Light vinaigrettes, yogurt	Heavy cream or butter

Chardonnay

Chardonnay varies greatly from being crisp with citrus and green apple flavors to complex with lots of oak and buttery - ness. It is important to know which type of Chardonnay you are drinking before you commit to pairings.

Crisp Chardonnay

	YES	*NO*
Seafood:	Most shellfish: raw or cooked and with light sauces	
Fish:	Higher fat, salmon, butterfish, poached or grilled	
Meat:	Chicken, turkey, veal	Lamb, beef
Cheese:	Goat herb cheese	Blue
Herbs & Spices:	Basil, chives, thyme, Saffron, marjoram, sage, tarragon	Cinnamon, Cilantro
Sauces:	In butter, olive oil, white sauce and mildly spiced sauces	Red or spicy

Chardonnay–Complex

	YES	*NO*
Fish:	Low to moderate fat, trout, halibut, swordfish–poached grilled or baked	Mackerel, tuna
Meat:	Chicken, veal, lamb or beef– light sauces	Squab
Cheese:	Asiago, fontina, mozzarella	Blue
Herbs & Spices:	Rosemary, oregano, ginger, saffron, tarragon, bay leaf	Cinnamon, cloves, Curry, ginger
Sauces:	Butter, cream, mayonnaise	Barbecue, salsa

Pinot Noir

Rich and complex character and texture with cherry, berry and violet aromas. Pairings are matched to medium-full bodied Pinot Noir with some depth.

	YES	NO
Seafood:	Scallops, crab, shrimp, abalone	Oysters
Fish:	Flounder, sole, salmon, tuna swordfish	Smoked fish
Meat:	All types of meat & poultry	
Cheese:	Brie, feta, jack, teleme	Cheddar, aged gouda
Herbs & Spices:	Basil, sage, oregano, fennel seed, balsamic vinegar, nutmeg, garlic	Cilantro, curry Cumin
Sauces:	Red wine, butter, mustard	Cream
Desserts:	Chocolate cakes and truffles	

Cabernet Sauvignon

A full-flavored wine with a very distinct character. Aromas and flavors of chocolate, spice, vanilla, cassis, and currant. Pairings are matched to a rich Cabernet Sauvignon.

	YES	NO
Fish:	Fish stews and cioppino salmon	Oysters, sole
Meat:	Steak, meatloaf, stew, barbecue ribs or chicken	Pork, veal
Cheese:	Aged goat & provolone sharp cheddar, blue	Jack, Swiss
Herbs & Spices:	Black pepper, rosemary, spearmint	Cilantro, cumin
	Garlic, aniseed	
Sauces:	Meat stock reduction, red wine, soy	Citrus, vinegar
Desserts:	Dark chocolate	

Merlot

A favorite that is fruity with a velvety texture. Aromas and flavors of plum, cherry, berry, vanilla. Pairings are matched to medium-bodied Merlot.

	YES	*NO*
Fish:	Fish stews and cioppino, blackened fish	
Meat:	Most types of meat & poultry, with a wine or brown sauce	
Cheese:	Most semi-soft, semi-hard	Sharp cheddar
Herbs & Spices:	Black pepper, rosemary, spearmint, oregano, basil, aniseed	Cilantro, cumin
Sauces:	Meat stock reduction, red wine, soy	Citrus, vinegar
Desserts:	Dark chocolate anything	

Zinfandel

A flavorful red wine with lots of fruit and spice. Aromas and flavors of black pepper, raspberries and blackberries. Pairings are matched to medium-bodied Zinfandel.

	YES	*NO*
Seafood:	Scallops, crab, abalone, shrimp–spiced red sauce	Raw oysters
Fish:	Most types of fish-mildly spiced in red/brown sauce	Sole, sushi
Meat:	Most types of meat and poultry, especially lamb	Pheasant, veal
Cheese:	Aged goat & provolone, sharp cheddar, blue	Jack, Swiss
Herbs & Spices:	Black pepper, rosemary, spearmint, garlic, cinnamon	Cilantro, cumin
Sauces:	Balsamic, mint, tomato	Butter, citrus
Desserts:	Dark chocolate anything	

TASTING NOTES ALONG THE WINE ROAD

Tasting Notes Along the Wine Road

Tasting Notes Along the Wine Road

Tasting Notes Along the Wine Road

Tasting Notes Along the Wine Road

Tasting Notes Along the Wine Road

For Additional Copies...

Like additional copies of this cookbook? Complete this order form and phone, mail, fax or e-mail to:

Russian River Wine Road
P.O. Box 46 Healdsburg, CA 95448
Telephone: (800) 723-6336 Fax: (707) 433-4374
Our web site: <www.wineroad.com>

Name_____

Address_____

Address_____

City_____State____Zip_____
( ) Copies @ $7.95 ea. & $2. S&H   Total_____
Credit Card (please circle):   MasterCard   Visa

_____Expires_____

Signature_____

COME BACK REAL SOON !

RUSSIAN RIVER RIVER WINE ROAD